AF527515

V for Vaccine

First published in India in 2021 by HarperCollins Children's Books
An imprint of HarperCollins Publishers
A-75, Sector 57, Noida, Uttar Pradesh 201301, India
www.harpercollins.co.in

2 4 6 8 10 9 7 5 3 1

Text © HarperCollins Publishers India 2021
Illustrations © HarperCollins Publishers India 2021

P-ISBN: 978-93-5422-418-8
E-ISBN: 978-93-5422-424-9

While every effort has been made to ensure the accuracy of the facts presented in the book, the publishers are not in any way liable for any errors that might have crept in.

All rights reserved. No part of this publication may be reproduced, stored in a retrieval system, or transmitted, in any form or by any means, electronic, mechanical, photocopying, recording or otherwise, without the prior permission of the publishers.

Design and layout in Gotham Rounded 10pt/ 15
by Isha Nagar, Delhi, India

Printed and bound in India by Thomson Press India Ltd.

V for Vaccine

A One-shot Introduction to Vaccines!

Illustrated by
Isha Nagar

HarperCollins*Children's Books*

We're

Veni, Vidi and Vici!

And most of all, we love talking about other things that start with V...like Vaccines!

What is a vaccine?

A vaccine is a type of medicine that helps prevent illness.

How is a vaccine different from other medicines?

Some medicines are meant to be taken after you fall sick. For example, if you have a fever, you can take medicines to help you get better. Vaccines teach your body to recognize and fight certain germs that make you ill, such as chickenpox or measles, so that you don't get sick.

Why do we need vaccines?

Germs like bacteria and viruses can cause infectious diseases that spread very easily. Vaccination is one of the best ways to prevent this. When enough people are vaccinated, these diseases can't spread anymore. We have even managed to get rid of some diseases, like smallpox, by vaccinating people.

How are vaccines given?

In most cases, vaccines are given by an injection in the arm or leg, but they can also be given as drops to swallow or a spray in the nose.

What is vaccination?

The process of giving or getting a vaccine is called vaccination. This is also called immunization, because vaccines give you immunity or protection from certain diseases caused by germs.

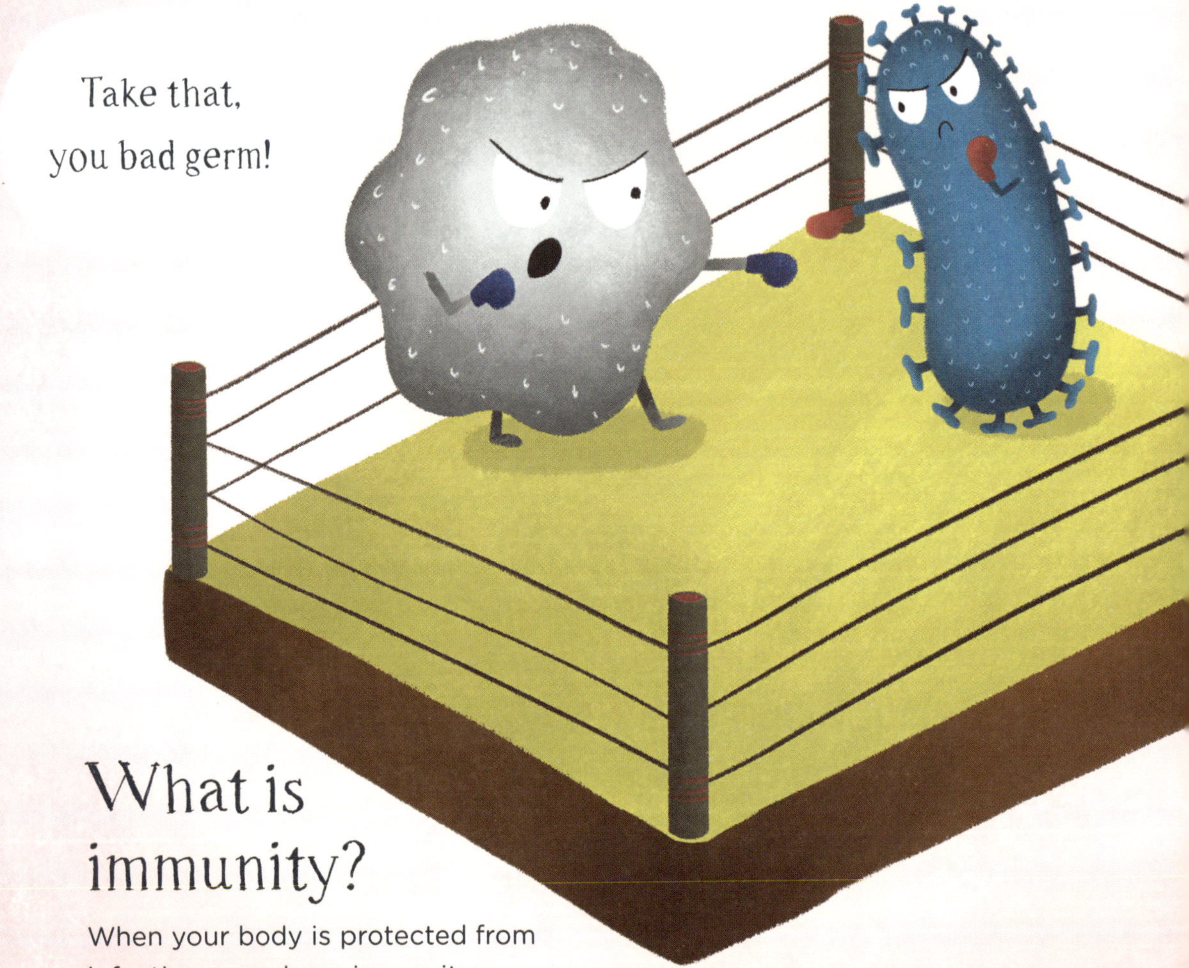

What is immunity?

When your body is protected from infections, you have immunity or protection. Our bodies protect us in many ways, using the immune system.

What is the immune system?

The immune system consists of different parts of the body, such as cells and organs, all working together to protect us from bacteria, viruses and other germs that can make us sick.

Your body knows how to protect you from some diseases from the time you're born. For example, your skin prevents certain germs from entering your body. Our bodies also have ways of recognizing when something is foreign, even if we haven't come across it before. This is known as innate immunity. Another form of immunity is acquired immunity, which people develop from being exposed to different germs.

I eat healthy food to build my immunity!

What are antibodies?

When harmful substances - like viruses, bacteria or other germs - enter our bodies, the immune system recognizes these 'invaders'. It fights them off by producing substances called antibodies.

An antibody is a protein that's shaped a little like a Y. When a virus, bacteria or germ enters your body, the immune system makes antibodies in response to the germ. These antibodies can attack the germs directly, or act indirectly by getting other parts of the immune system to respond. Antibodies are one of the most important elements of our immune system.

Your immune system also has a great memory! It remembers these germs so that the next time they try to attack, your body knows the right kind of antibodies to produce.

What do vaccines do?

Vaccines are like infections, except that they don't make you sick. Instead, the immune system thinks that a germ has arrived and responds to protect you. Vaccines are a clever way of teaching your body how to fight off germs that haven't tried to attack you yet, so that the first time these germs try to make you feel sick, your immune system is already prepared!

Do vaccines cure diseases?

By helping you develop immunity to a disease, vaccines stop you from falling sick in the first place. This means that they don't cure diseases, they stop them from happening. This is great not just for the person who has been vaccinated but for their family and community as well because there will be fewer sick people around to spread the disease. No cure, but lots of reduction.

Where did vaccines come from?

The idea of using a small, weak dose of a virus, germ or toxin to build your immunity has actually been around for centuries! For smallpox, this practice was followed in different parts of the world, including China, Turkey, India and some countries in Africa. However, the kind of vaccines that are used today were developed around 1796.

When was the first vaccine created?

An English scientist named Edward Jenner is known as the inventor of the first vaccine. Around 1796, Edward Jenner used material from cowpox as a vaccine in order to give people immunity from smallpox. Soon, this vaccine was given to people around the world. Thanks to the smallpox vaccine, this deadly disease is no longer a threat!

How are vaccines made?

There are many steps taken to make sure that a vaccine is safe and works before it is ready to be used by people. Vaccines contain a number of ingredients, but the most important is a part or whole of the germ that causes illness. These are called antigens.

What is an antigen?

The antigen is the element of the vaccine that triggers the body's immune response. It is usually a small part of a bacteria or virus. This antigen teaches the immune system how to recognize and fight off the bacteria or virus. The antigen cannot give you the disease – it just tells your body what to look out for.

What happens after a vaccine is created?

After a vaccine is created, it has to be tested so that scientists can prove that it works. All vaccines are tested using similar processes, so that doctors and scientists can be sure that they are safe and effective to use. Once the right antigen is identified and scientists have carried out tests in their laboratories, the vaccines are tested, first on animals and then on human volunteers.

This happens in three different stages. Thousands of people receive the trial vaccine, and scientists monitor them to make sure that the vaccine is safe, makes the right kind of immune response and protects from illness. These trials often happen in different countries at the same time. Next, scientists and experts review the results from all these trials. If the vaccine is shown to be safe and to produce immunity, it is approved.

What are some popular vaccines?

Lots of vaccines have been approved and been in use for many years, all over the world. For example, there are vaccines for diseases such as chickenpox, measles, mumps, polio and tetanus. Some of these diseases used to be very dangerous, but thanks to vaccination, we can stay safe and develop immunity to them from a very young age.

Why is there so much talk of vaccines currently?

You might have heard a lot of discussion about vaccines recently. That's because of COVID-19, a disease that is currently affecting lots of people around the world. COVID-19 is caused by the coronavirus, a kind of virus. It causes symptoms like a cough, shortness of breath and fever, and in some cases it can make people very sick. COVID-19 also spreads very easily from person to person.

Since COVID-19 is a new disease, when it first started affecting people, we didn't have a way to prevent it. But scientists and researchers all over the world have worked together to share information and learn more about the virus, so that they can develop a vaccine. Thanks to their hard work, vaccines for COVID-19 have been developed and tested in many countries. In several places, including India, vaccination against COVID-19 has already begun.

For widespread diseases like COVID-19, it's impossible to vaccinate everyone in the country at the same time. That's why vaccines are often given to people in different stages. First, doctors, nurses and people who work in hospitals are given the vaccine. This is so that they can stay protected while they continue to go to work every day to keep their patients safe!

Are there different types of vaccines?

There are many different types of vaccines. All of them teach your body how to develop immunity by using a weakened or dead form of the bacteria or virus that causes the disease. As we learn more about science and develop new technologies, new forms of vaccines are being created. Instead of including a part or whole of the virus or bacteria, these vaccines give your body messages about how to make the antigen, to which the immune system responds.

How do I get a vaccine?

You've probably been vaccinated before! Most children receive vaccinations from the time they're very young. Vaccines are normally given at an immunization clinic. You usually get a vaccine in the form of an injection, but a few vaccines are in the form of drops or a nasal spray.

Do vaccines hurt?

You might feel a stinging or pricking feeling when you receive the vaccine. That's normal, and it is generally over very quickly. The doctor or nurse might ask you to take a deep breath before you take the vaccine, because this helps your body relax. Getting a vaccine might feel uncomfortable, but it's one of the best ways to keep you and the people around you healthy.

What happens after *I* take a vaccine?

After you are vaccinated, you might not feel any different at all. Sometimes, you might notice a small bump or some redness at the spot where you got vaccinated.

As the vaccine starts working, you could also feel a bit tired or have a low fever. This is normal, and is actually a sign that your body is beginning to build immunity.

Why do *I* have to take some vaccines more than once?

Some vaccines are designed to be taken in multiple doses – the same way you have to take some medicines for more than one day in order to get better. Sometimes, you have to receive booster doses after a few years, to make sure your body has the right immunity levels.

In some cases, like for the flu, kids and adults have to get vaccinated every year. This is because the flu is an especially tricky illness! There are lots of different viruses that can cause the flu, and so the vaccine needs to be 'updated' regularly to make sure you can stay immune.

I'm ready for my second dose!

Are vaccines just for kids?

Most vaccinations happen when you're very young, so that you're protected from these harmful diseases from as early as possible. But vaccines aren't just for kids! Kids and adults can take annual vaccines like the flu vaccine. There are also new vaccines being developed every day, as scientists and doctors learn more about how to build immunity. When new vaccines are made, who gets them depends on the kind of illness they prevent.

Can animals get vaccines too?

Vaccines aren't just for humans! If you have a pet, like a cat or a dog, they need to be vaccinated too. Animals get vaccinated at the vet, just like humans visit the doctor. Vaccines for animals work the same way as they do for you: they help your pets build immunity and keep them from catching or spreading harmful diseases.

Can everyone get vaccinated?

Just like other medicines, all vaccines work a little bit differently. Some vaccines can be given to people of all ages, from newborns to adults. Others can only be given to people of a certain age. For example, some vaccines are only recommended for people above the age of 18. Some vaccines can't be given to pregnant women, or to people who have certain illnesses.

If you can get vaccinated, it also helps to keep the people around you safe!

What are some other ways to stay healthy?

Vaccines are one of the most important ways to keep you and the people around you safe from diseases. But, they're not the only way to stay healthy!

- You can make sure your body and immune system are strong by eating a balanced diet with lots of fruit and vegetables.
- It's always a good idea to get a lot of exercise and stay active.
- You can keep yourself and the people around you safe by following basic rules of hygiene, like washing your hands before meals and after going to the toilet.

When new diseases develop, it can take a while for scientists to find a cure. That's why it's always important to protect yourself and others from falling sick. There are lots of easy ways to do this!

- If you have a cough or a cold, remember to sneeze or cough into a tissue, and then throw away the tissue.
- If you're unwell, it's a good idea to stay home and rest until you get better, so that you don't infect others.

For diseases like COVID-19, you might also be given specific advice by your parents, teachers or doctors - like wearing a mask and practicing social distancing. Wearing a mask helps keep away the germs that can be released when you cough or sneeze. Social distancing is another simple way of making sure that contagious diseases like COVID-19 don't spread as easily. Following guidelines like these is the best thing you can do to stay safe!

And now it's time to bid goodbye to

Veni, Vidi and Vici

WE CAME, WE SAW AND WE WILL CONQUER

viruses and sickness
with the right VACCINE!

Thank you!

We would like to thank **Dr. Gagandeep Kang** for her valuable inputs on the content of this book.

Dr. Kang is a Professor of Microbiology at the Wellcome Trust Research Laboratory, Division of Gastrointestinal Sciences at the Christian Medical College, Vellore. She has worked on the development and use of vaccines for rotaviruses, cholera and typhoid. She is the first woman working in India to be elected a Fellow of the Royal Society of London.

Have you heard of Covie the germ?

THE GERM ACADEMY

By Rea Malhotra Mukhtyar and Shahena Zaveri

Covie's the baddest of the baddies. Trained by evil masterminds at The Germ Academy, he won't stop causing havoc until he's the World's Best Infection and nothing's coming in his way!

...or so he thinks.

Enter The Soap Squad. This bottled brigade takes pride in keeping the planet squeaky clean, even if it means squashing a few hopes and dreams along the way.

What happens when their two worlds collide? Come find out in this very timely story that's a little bit creepy, a little bit bubbly, and a whole lot of fun!

Give it your
best shot!

I'm ______________________________

and this is my VACCINE CARD!

My Vaccine Card

Name of the Vaccine	Vaccination Against	Age	Booster doses